Piano Music of

Africa

and the

African Diaspora

Compiled and Edited by
William H. Chapman Nyaho

Volume 1
Early Intermediate

MUSIC DEPARTMENT

OXFORD
UNIVERSITY PRESS

OXFORD
UNIVERSITY PRESS

198 Madison Avenue, New York, NY, 10016, USA
Great Clarendon Street, Oxford OX2 6DP, England

Oxford University Press is a department of the University of Oxford.
It furthers the University's aim of excellence in research, scholarship,
and education by publishing worldwide

Oxford New York
Auckland Bangkok Buenos Aires Cape Town Chennai
Dar es Salaam Delhi Hong Kong Istanbul Karachi Kolkata
Kuala Lumpur Madrid Melbourne Mexico City Mumbai Nairobi
São Paulo Shanghai Taipei Tokyo Toronto

ISBN 978-0-19-386822-9

Music origination by
Enigma Music Production Services, Amersham, Bucks, UK
Printed in Great Britain on acid-free paper

Contents

Foreword

The need for piano music written by Black composers and designed at least initially for pedagogical functions has been on the minds of piano teachers for many years. The most celebrated composers have mainly written large recital works and that is why the piano music in this graded collection is a welcome addition to the repertoire.

The short history on graded anthologies by Black composers would include the *Diatonica Harmonica* by the Afro-British violinist and pianist, George Bridgetower, but this is an ethnically innocent means of teaching scales and in making their application more interesting through harmonic settings. There is also an anthology of original and arranged works for piano by the nineteenth-century Brazilian of African descent, José Maurício Nunes García. In the absence of such repertoire, piano teachers created works for their own students—the case of Florence Price being a major example, but such works, if published at all, were allowed to go out of print quite soon.

Now we have a solution, one that will immediately address the interests not just of pianists and pedagogues, but past that point will also serve excellently for music scholars and enthusiasts who are interested in the kind of new aesthetic horizons, harmonic practices, and rhythmic and metric challenges this literature offers. A new world of music is coming into our awareness, and in many instances, it is not just new music and viewpoints, but new composers. Alongside the cherished patriarchs are individuals who consciously endow their works with African perspectives and whose music we have never seen in print.

While many composers live and work in Africa, the vast geographic representation outside of Africa in this collection is symptomatic of the extent of the Diaspora. African presence is felt in music around the world. By including Bangambula (resident in China), we are reminded of Africans in Asia, whose history is a thousand years old, dating back to the importation of xylophone-type instruments to Africa from the South Pacific. As for Europe, there were enough Blacks in eighteenth-century France to create an all-Black regiment of 1,000 men, serving under the leadership of the Chevalier de Saint-Georges, composer, violinist, and champion fencer who came from Guadeloupe. In Portugal, Vicente Lusitano, a sixteenth-century choral composer and music theorist of African descent, developed a widely-known treatise on the diatonic, chromatic, and enharmonic genera. In the Caribbean and South America, where ethnic identification is not as easily determined since national identity is given priority over racial background, African influences are present in almost all types of music.

Due to the extensive and unconscious absorption of African music in the Diaspora, the music of this historically significant piano collection—much of which is officially new to the repertoire—is far more familiar and recognizable than anticipated.

Dominique-René de Lerma, Chief Advisor
The Rachel Elizabeth Barton Foundation

Preface

The vast—and until now generally unavailable—repertoire of piano music of Africa and its Diaspora appears in myriad forms and styles, from simple to virtuosic. This compilation brings to light music that has remained in manuscript form, music that has been out of print, and music by present day composers that is not widely circulated. Furthermore, this collection should serve as a refreshing teaching aid, offering something new and stimulating for students. Graded in order of difficulty, the works get successively more complicated in each volume and may present challenges to some students at particular levels, which in many instances may be overcome by following the performance notes. African oral, aural, and corporal learning techniques—such as singing the rhythmic and melodic passages, repeatedly clapping or drumming rhythms, dancing, and moving to embody musical gestures—may be very beneficial in learning and interpreting this music effectively. Using this collection as a vehicle for diversity, teachers should encourage students not only to examine their own musical traditions but also those of other cultures. In addition to private piano instructors, institutions of higher education may find this collection quite useful as a supplement to keyboard literature courses and in piano pedagogy classes on the topics of learning styles and multicultural influences in music.

There are some renowned composers not represented here for several reasons. Either their estates demanded prohibitive royalties, or establishing contact for permission proved too difficult. In a few instances, I did not include works by well-known composers simply because they are already well in circulation.

On a personal note, I would like to honor my parents for affirming my appreciation of African traditional music and also my love of piano music. I am particularly thrilled to discover wonderful works by composers of Africa and Its Diaspora that reflect the intercultural nature of my upbringing. I am deeply indebted to the composers, colleagues, family, and friends who have been very encouraging and cooperative in this groundbreaking project, and it is my sincere hope that this compilation will lead to an even greater spurt in research on composers of Africa and Its Diaspora. My dream is that this piano music will become a regular part of recitals, piano festivals, and competitions.

Lastly, I invite and encourage you to take a journey through these works; to experience the musical fusion of Africa and the African Diaspora; and to explore new ways of learning and performing piano music.

WILLIAM H. CHAPMAN NYAHO, 2007

Acknowledgements

I would like to acknowledge the following people who have contributed in so many ways to this project: Jane Efua Chapman Nyaho, Daniel Chapman Nyaho, my family, my teachers, Howard Cooper, Dr. Maya Angelou, Margaret Courtney-Clark, Louise Toppin, Akin Euba, Brian Hill, Todd Waldman, John Kubiniec, Kirsten Hodge, Christopher Johnson, the staff of the Music Department at Oxford University Press, Dominique-René de Lerma, Martha Hilley, Myrna Capp, Guy Bowman, Jan Jones, Calvin Sharpe, Garth Fagan, Dr. Maxine Mimms, Myrtle David, Halim El-Dabh, David Badagnani, Oswald Russell, Robin Williams, Bill Zick at AfriClassical.com, and Howard Dodson at the Schomburg Center for Research in Black Culture, and the Center for Black Music Research.

Composer Biographies

Valerie Capers
Jazz pianist, composer, and arranger, Valerie Capers received her schooling at the New York Institute for the Education of the Blind and her Bachelor's and Master's degrees from the Juilliard School of Music. She was awarded an honorary doctorate from Susquehanna University. Capers has served on the faculty of Manhattan School of Music and is Professor Emeritus at the Bronx Community College of CUNY. Capers appears regularly on the national and international scene with her trio and ensemble in concert halls, festivals, clubs, and universities. She has written cantatas, operatorios, a song cycle for voice, piano, and cello, and a suite of piano pieces titled *Portraits in Jazz*.

Halim El-Dabh
Composer, performer, ethnomusicologist, and educator, Halim El-Dabh is internationally regarded as one of Egypt's foremost living composers. Presently Professor Emeritus at Kent State University's School of Music, El-Dabh studied piano, *derabucca* (goblet-shaped ceramic drum), and composition at Cairo University, the University of New Mexico, New England Conservatory of Music, and Brandeis University. El-Dabh assisted Igor Stravinsky and studied with Aaron Copland and Irving Fine. His wide ranging ethnomusicological research has led to a unique fusion of contemporary compositional techniques and Ancient Egyptian, African, and Middle Eastern traditional music. His numerous musical and dramatic works have been performed throughout Africa, Asia, Europe, and the Americas. His works for piano include *Mekta' in the art of Kita'*, *Osmo-Symbiotic* for two pianos, *Table Dance*, and *Mosaic* for piano and percussion and a piano concerto, *Surrr-Rah*.

Robert Mawuena Kwami
Ghanaian composer and educator Robert Mawuena Kwami was raised in a musical environment. He studied at Achimota School and Reading Univiersity, and then later earned his Master's degree and Ph.D. at the University of London, Institute of Education. He has taught in various locations including the University of Ghana, Cross River State University in Nigeria, and the University of Pretoria in South Africa. His wide-ranging publications focused on music education and its practice in Africa. Kwami's piano compositions range from simple teaching pieces to works that are a fusion of art music and Ghanaian traditional and popular music. His works for piano include *Agbadza*, *January Dance*, *Elegy*, and *6 Piano Pieces*.

Kwabena Nketia
Ghanaian composer, musicologist, and educator Kwabena Nketia received early musical training in Ghana and studied piano, musicology, and composition at various institutions such as Birkeck College, University of London, Trinity College of Music, Columbia University, Juilliard School of Music, and Northwestern University. Nketia returned to teach at the University of Ghana and became Director of the Institute of African Studies. He also taught at UCLA and the University of Pittsburgh. Nketia advocates a contemporary compositional technique, a fusion between folk and contemporary music. He has transcribed several traditional songs, has composed several choral works, and has written extensively for Western instruments, traditional African instruments, and a combination of both.

Nkeiru Okoye

Composer, pianist, and conductor Nkeiru Okoye received her degrees from Oberlin College and Rutgers University and studied under composers such as Noel DaCosta and Ronald Senator. She was the recipient of a Ford-Mellon Foundation grant for ground-breaking research on Black women composers, through which she authored *A Finding Aid for the Works of Black Women Composers* and began a collection of works by Black women composers for the Oberlin College Conservatory Library. She has been Protégé Composer for the Detroit Symphony Orchestra's African-American Composer Symposium. Okoye's compositions are written for orchestra, chamber ensemble, and piano, and are a collage of American, West African, and European musical traditions. Her piano works include *African Sketches*, a suite of pieces consisting of *Village Children at Play, Dusk,* and *Dancing Barefoot in the Rain.*

Christian Onyeji

Nigerian composer, pianist, choreographer, conductor, and music and theater director Christian Onyeji holds degrees in composition from the University of Nigeria and the University of Pretoria, South Africa. He is currently Senior Lecturer and Acting Head of the Department of Music, University of Nigeria. Having contributed several important articles to ethnomusicology and education journals, Onyeji specializes in "Research-Composition," a modern approach to art music composition that entails application of ethnomusicological procedures in the composition of modern African art music. He has written for symphony orchestra, piano, and choirs. His choral music appears in *World Carols for Choirs* published by Oxford University Press, and his piano works include *Oga, Ufie I, II, III.*

Florence B. Price

Florence B. Price was the first African-American composer, concert pianist, and organist to reach national recognition. Price studied at the New England Conservatory of Music and later taught at the Cotton-Plant Arkadelphia Academy and Shorter College in Little Rock before becoming Head of the Music Department at Clark University in Atlanta. After a return to Arkansas, she moved to Chicago where she eventually became known nationally and internationally as a composer and concert pianist. Price has the distinction of being the first African American to have her work performed by leading orchestras such as the Chicago Symphony Orchestra. During her career, Price wrote over three hundred compositions, including symphonies, concertos, chamber works, art songs, and settings of spirituals for voice and piano. Her works for piano range from several short teaching pieces to larger works such as *Sonata in E minor, Fantasie Negre,* and *Dances in the Canebrakes.*

Isak Roux

Isak Roux is a South African composer-pianist who studied at University of Natal; studied with composers such as Kevin Volans, Ulrich Süsse, and Jürgen Bräuninger; and is presently teaching at the Waldorf School in Stutttgart. As composer Roux has participated in the International Composers Workshop in Amsterdam and Tonkünstlerfest in Baden-Württemberg. He has given recitals of his own works, performed concerts with pennywhistle virtuoso Jake Lerole, and appeared in numerous festivals in South Africa. Roux has also appeared with Ladysmith Black Mambazo as well as arranging and producing their Grammy nominated album No Boundaries. He has composed works for chamber ensemble, voice, and orchestra. Roux's piano works include *Music for Two Pianists; Preludes in African Rhythm, Home; African Miniatures (Music for Young Pianists); Dr. Kwela - Mr. Ragtime.*

Hale Smith

African-American composer, editor, and arranger Hale Smith first studied classical and jazz piano and then received his degrees in composition from the Cleveland Institute of Music. He taught at C.W. Post College (Long Island) and is Professor Emeritus at the University of Connecticut–Storrs. Smith has been an artistic consultant for the Black Music Repertory Ensemble at the Center for Black Music Research Columbia College in Chicago. He is also well known as an arranger and has worked prominently with jazz musicians such as Dizzy Gillespie, Chico Hamilton, Ahmad Jamal, Melba Liston, and Randy Weston. As editor, he has worked with major music publishers. As composer, he has written for orchestra, chorus, solo voice, chamber ensemble, and solo instruments. His piano works include *Faces in Jazz*, *Anticipations*, *introspections and reflections*, *Inventions*, *4 Mosaics*, and *Sonata*.

Ulysses Kay

African-American composer Ulysses Kay studied piano at the encouragement of his uncle, jazz legend Joe "King" Oliver, and later, William Grant Still. He studied with Bernard Rogers, Howard Hanson, Paul Hindemith, and Otto Luening at the University of Arizona, Eastman School of Music, Yale University, and Columbia University. Kay taught at Boston University, University of California–Los Angeles, Macalester College, and Brevard Music Center and was distinguished professor of theory and composition at Lehman College at CUNY. Kay spent a majority of his career composing commissions and scores for film and television. Kay's compositions include instrumental, chamber, orchestral, choral, dramatic, incidental, and commercial music. His piano music includes *Four Inventions*, *Two Nocturnes*, *Ten Short Essays* or *Ten Pieces for Children*, *Two Impromptus*, *Visions*, *Two Short Pieces for Piano Four-Hands*.

Bangambula Vindu

Congolese composer André Bangambula Vindu studied at the Conservatoire de Musique et d'Art Dramatique and the Institut National des Arts of the Université Nationale du Zaïre (INAUNZ) in Kinshasa. He received degrees from the Shanghai Conservatory of Music in China studying composition with Wang Qiang and Zhao Xiao-sheng. Vindu has lectured on music theory and saxophone at the INAUNZ and also served as head of the music department, assistant professor and leader of the experimental ensemble Maisha at the Centre d'Études et de Diffusion des Arts in Kinshasa. Vindu's recent positions have included teaching music in Hong Kong and Shanghai. He has also participated in international festivals and symposia throughout Europe, North America, Africa and Asia. His compositions include vocal, chamber, and orchestral works. He has also made arrangements of traditional Congolese Folksongs. His piano works include *Rêverie*; several fugues, and a suite.

Performance Notes

1. Kwela No. 1– Isak Roux
The articulations of this happy, light-hearted piece should be sharply defined. "Kwela" is derived from the Zulu term for "get up"—it is an invitation to dance. This style of music was primarily written for the pennywhistle and became popular internationally and used in many forms.

2. Tender Thought – Ulysses Kay
This piece should be played as lyrically as possible. Take care to bring out the middle voice particularly in mm. 16–24. Rests in mm. 31–3 in the bass are very important in articulating the meter of the piece.

3. My Scarf is Yellow – Hale Smith
Extra care should be given to the slurs and other articulations at the beginning. The rhythm should be exact in the middle section with precise releases at the end of the measures, such as in mm. 9, 11, and 15.

4. Dusk – Nkeiru Okoye
This was written after the passing of Noel DaCosta, Okoye's mentor and friend for a decade. The music is soulful, spiritual, and reflective, reflecting the spirituality of her departed teacher.

5. Piano Piece No. 2, Call and Response – Robert Mawuena Kwami
The practice of call and response in African traditional music is very common. As the title suggests, make sure the melodic lines in both hands are well shaped and projected. Pay close attention to slurs.

6. Soufiane – Halim El-Dabh
El-Dabh frequently draws on his Egyptian heritage for Soufiane. This piece uses a motive based on two very common Arabic tetrachords "Hijaz" and "Nahawand." The Middle Eastern sound is due to the Hijaz tetrachord with its augmented second surrounded by minor seconds. El-Dabh says, "*Soufiane* is to be performed with a deep introspective feeling as if connecting man to the universe."

7. Off-Beat Shorty – Hale Smith
Off-Beat Shorty comes from *Face of Jazz,* a set of twelve pieces for the young pianist. The piece emphasizes off beats and is designed to train the pianist to create a springing sound through a quick release of tension.

8. Ticklin' Toes – Florence B. Price
This light-hearted piece is best performed with strict observance of articulations. The character of the middle section is playful and deserves emphasis on the dynamics.

9. **Sweet Mister Jelly Roll** – Valerie Capers
This piece makes no attempt to imitate the piano style of the great Jelly Roll Morton, but rather tries to recreate in the simplest way the sound and style of ragtime piano. The left hand plays a simplified version of stride bass, a technique of ragtime and swing. Play this with spirit and humor, but always remember the words of Scott Joplin: "It is never right to play ragtime fast."

10. **Dancing Barefoot in the Rain** – Nkeiru Okoye
Okoye writes, "*Dancing Barefoot in the Rain* recalls the rainy season, from life in Enugu (a city in South East Nigeria). As children, whenever warm tropical drops filled the sky, my sister and I would run downstairs and across the courtyard surrounding our home to meet our playmates for an afternoon of slippery, barefoot fun." Taken from a suite called *African Sketches*, this piece needs a bright, joyous sound with articulations strictly observed, especially in the left hand, which should be active and playful in character.

11. **Lullaby** – Isak Roux
This is a simple, pentatonic cradle song that features the melodic structure of typical Zulu folk songs. The main melody is primarily projected in the left hand, and it should be played with emotion.

12. **The Monk** – Valerie Capers
Imitating the piano style of Thelonius Monk, bring out the open fifth and sevenths, the biting seconds, the off-balance accents, and the tightly clustered chords, and pay strict attention to all accents and phrase marks. In the mm. 7–9 there is a quote from Monk's famous blues work called *Straight No Chaser.*

13. **Lullaby** – Bangambula Vindu
This lullaby is inspired by Congolese folksong. It should be played in a deeply lyrical and expressive manner. The left hand phrases should be well shaped, and the right hand melody should be projected as if it were sung.

14. **Builsa Work Song** – J. H. Kwabena Nketia
This reflects the music and dance of the Builsa people from the northeastern part of Ghana. This is a bright, joyous version of one of their folksongs. The opening short-long rhythms should snap, and the sounds of the bass notes and silences of the rests should feel percussive.

15. **Ufie III** – Christian Onyeji
Ufie is a synthesis of dance, polyrhythm, and texture, which incorporates stylistic features of *Ufie*, a generic large wooden slit drum, written for a new medium, the piano. It is a three-movement work of contrasting tempi that features a ten-note scale made up of two pentatonic scales derived from the *Ukom* music of the Ngwa community. This work should be played in a driving drum-like manner. Care should be given to the dynamic markings; they make for a dramatic performance.

Piano Music of

Africa

and the

African Diaspora

1. Kwela No. 1

From *African Miniatures for Young Pianists*

ISAK ROUX (SOUTH AFRICA)
(b. 1959)

This collection © 2007, Oxford University Press, Inc, assigned to Oxford University Press 2010.

Printed in the UK

2. Tender Thought

From *Ten Short Essays*

ULYSSES KAY (USA)
(1917–95)

poco rit.

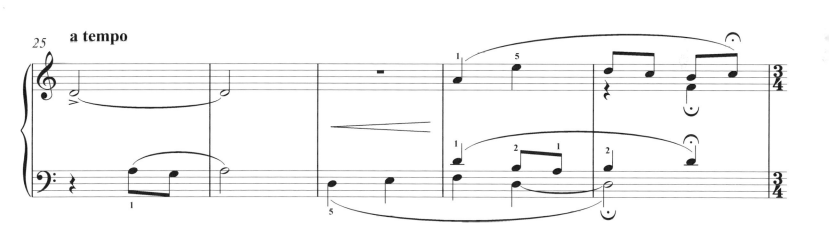

a tempo

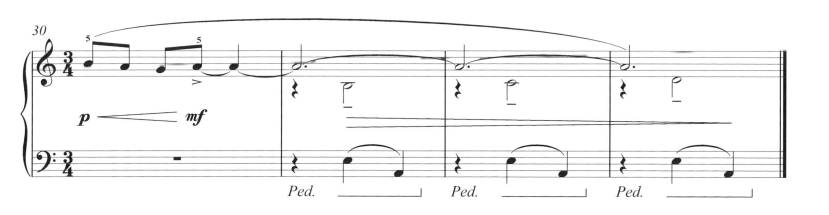

Ped.   Ped.   Ped.

3. My Scarf is Yellow

From *Faces of Jazz*

HALE SMITH (USA)
(b. 1925)

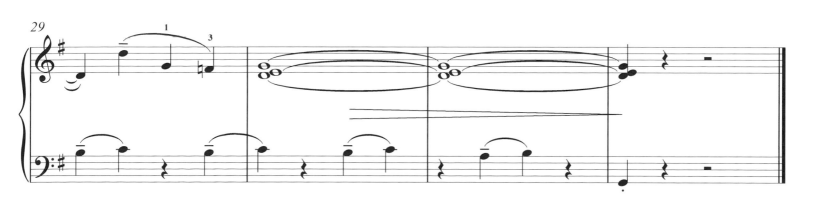

4. Dusk

From *African Sketches*

NKEIRU OKOYE (NIGERIA/USA)
(b. 1972)

dedicated to Ethlena Chambers

5. Piano Piece No. 2, Call and Response

From *Six Piano Pieces*

ROBERT MAWUENA KWAMI (GHANA)
(1954–2004)

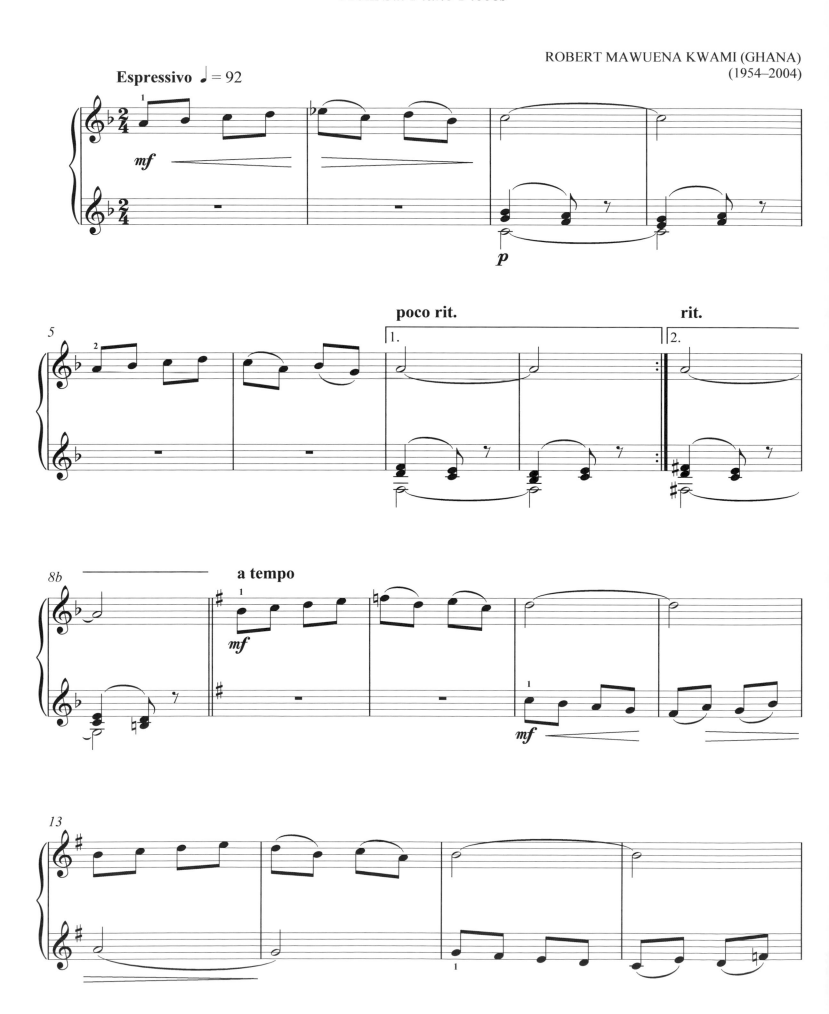

6. Soufiane صوفيان

From *Mekta' in the Art of Kita' Book 2*

HALIM EL-DABH (EGYPT)
(b. 1921)

7. Off-Beat Shorty

From *Faces of Jazz*

HALE SMITH (USA)
(b. 1925)

8. Ticklin' Toes

FLORENCE B. PRICE (USA)
(1887–1953)

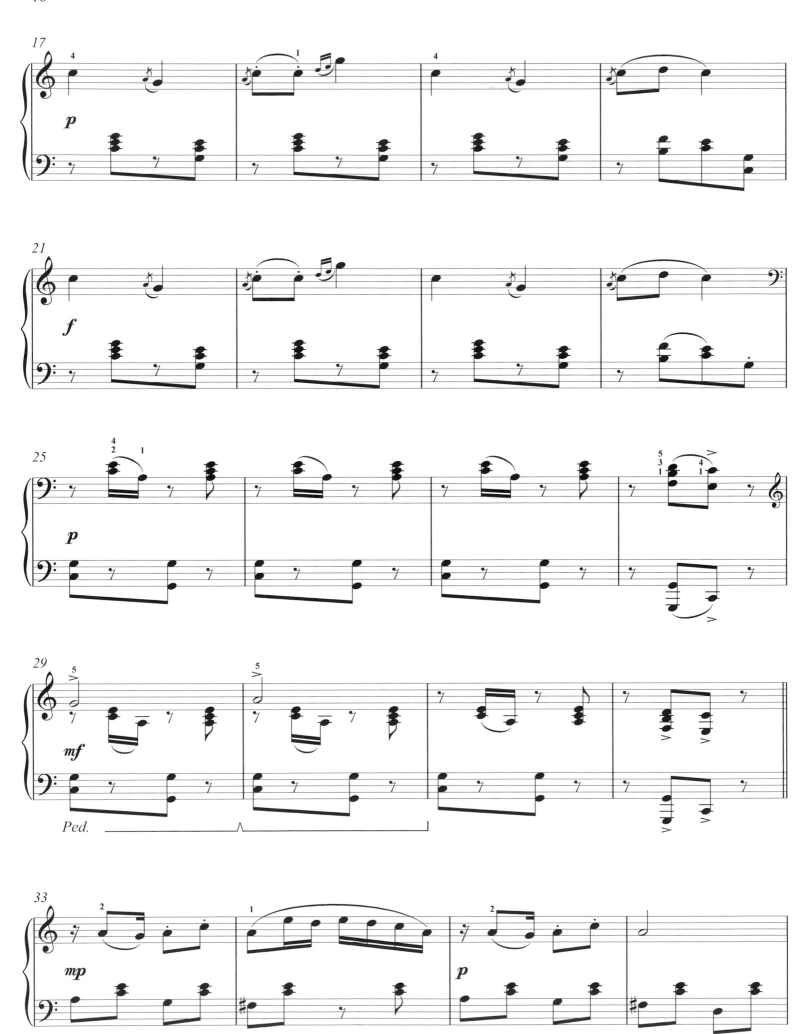

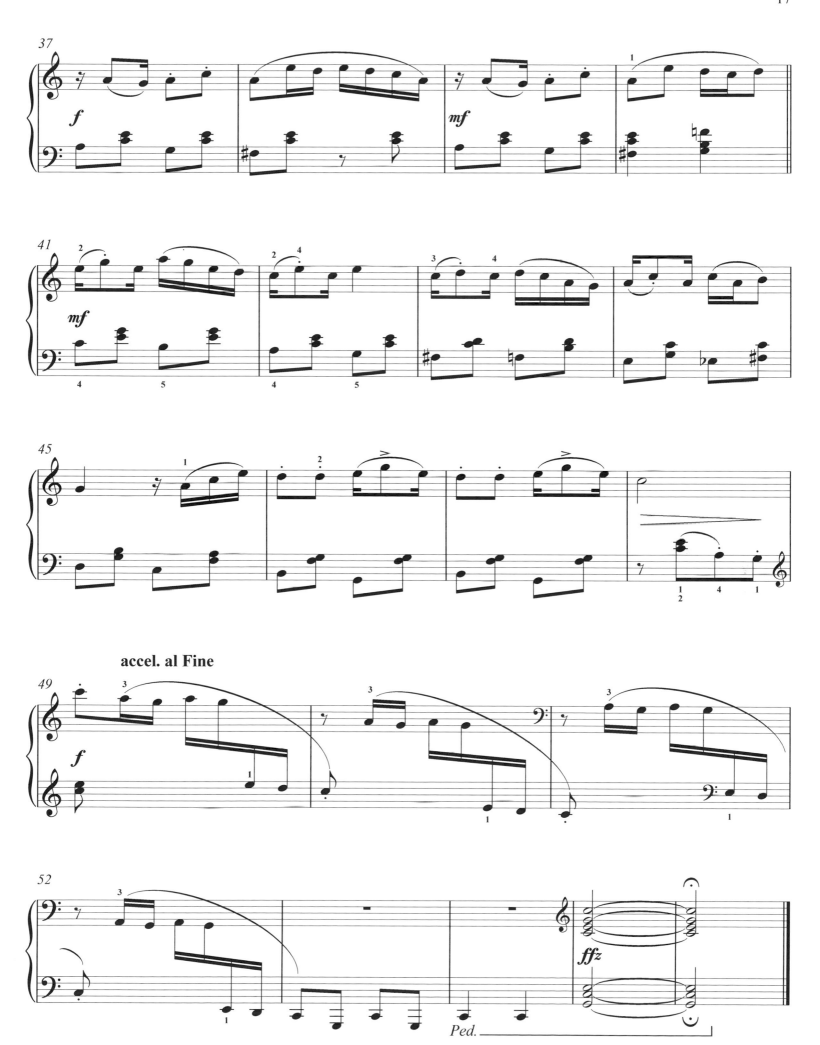

9. Sweet Mister Jelly Roll

From *Portraits in Jazz*

VALERIE CAPERS (USA)
(b. 1935)

last time to Coda ⊕

⊕ CODA

D. 𝄋 al Coda

10. Dancing Barefoot in the Rain

From African Sketches

NKEIRU OKOYE (NIGERIA/USA)
(b. 1972)

Lively, light, and dancelike ♩ = 120

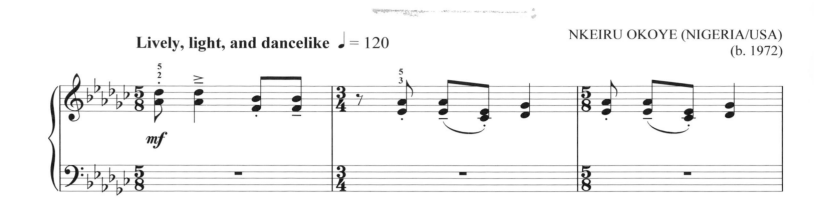

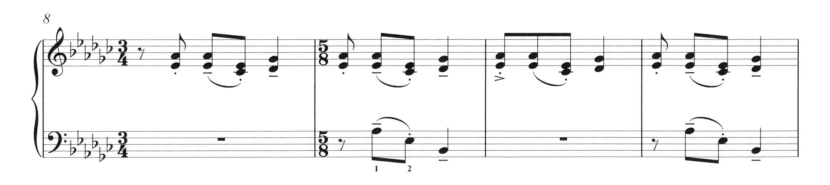

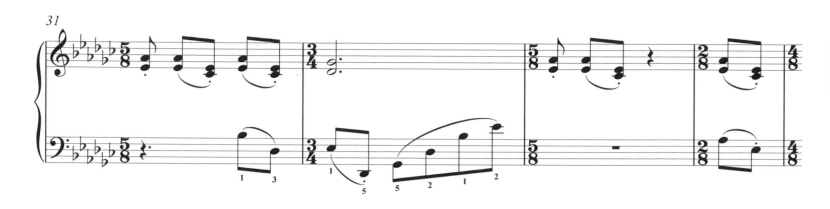

11. Lullaby

From *Preludes in African Rhythm*

Lento e molto rubato ♪ = 72

ISAK ROUX (SOUTH AFRICA)
(b. 1959)

12. The Monk

From *Portraits in Jazz*

VALERIE CAPERS (USA)
(b. 1935)

13. Lullaby

From *Suite for Piano*

BANGAMBULA VINDU (CONGO)
(b. 1953)

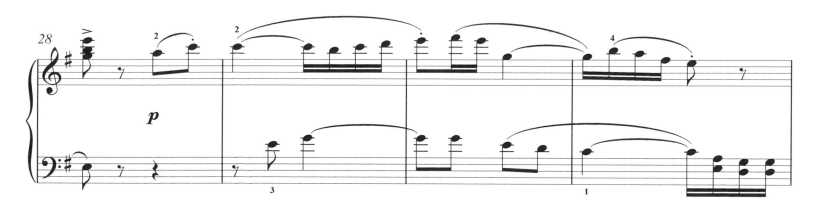

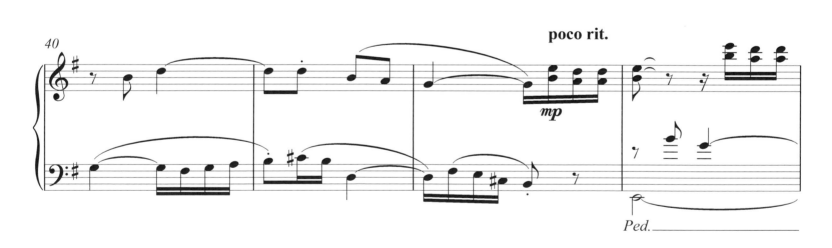

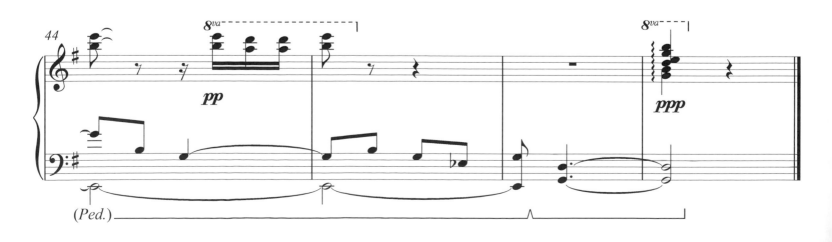

14. Builsa Work Song

From *Twelve Pedagogical Pieces*

J. H. KWABENA NKETIA (GHANA)
(b. 1921)

15. Ufie III

CHRISTIAN ONYEJI (NIGERIA)
(b. 1967)

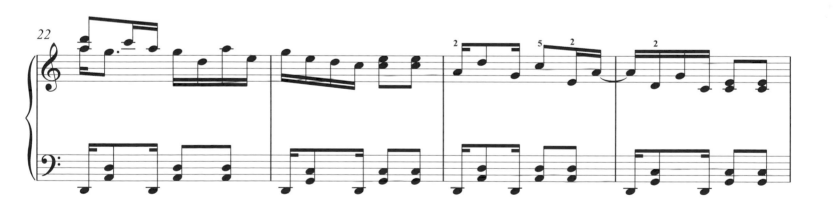

last time to Coda ⊕

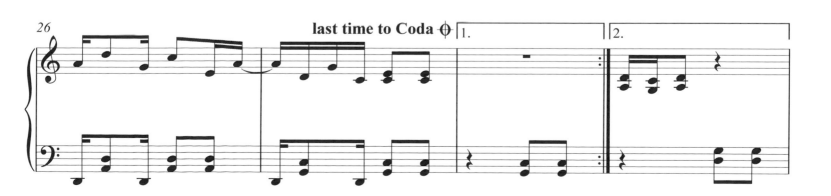

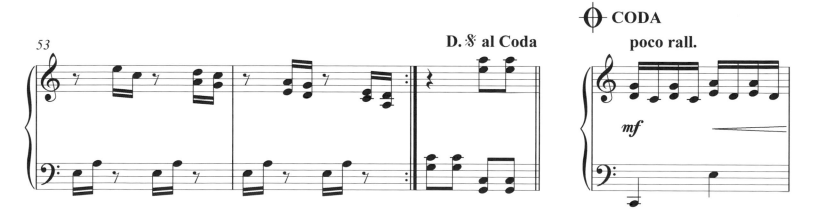

CODA

D. 𝄋 al Coda

poco rall.

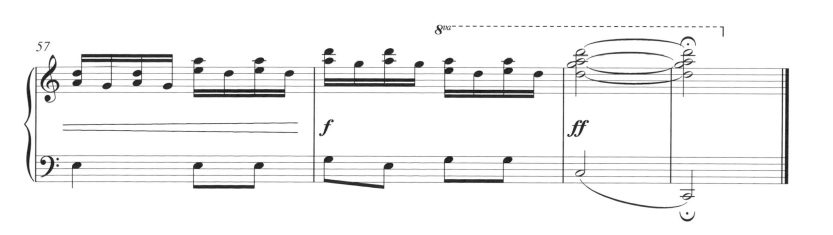